CONTENTS

I.

WHEN I AM LIFTED UP

I, when I am lifted up from the earth, will draw all men to myself. —John 12:32

THIS word of our Lord was spoken at the time when some Greeks came asking to see Him. We may suppose that, like the Athenians of whom Paul writes, they shared the general desire of the Greeks to "hear some new thing." Perhaps they wanted this Teacher to visit Greece and join in the discussions of the Stoa at Athens. But this, natural as it might seem, is not the way in which the Saviour of the world will become known as Saviour. The corn of wheat must fall into the ground and die if it is to bear fruit. The Saviour must be lifted up on the Cross if He is to draw the nations to Himself. It is not just His teaching or His person which can provide the mercy-seat to which all the nations may come for pardon and reconciliation.

5

That mercy-seat is provided in His dying. (Note that the Greek word *hilasterion,* translated as "expiation" in Romans 3:25, RSV, is the word used for the "mercy-seat" in the Greek version of Exodus and Leviticus, and in Hebrews 9:5.)

To this one mercy-seat, established by God, the nations will be drawn. Only here can the chasm between Jew and Gentile be healed. It is only "in the blood of Christ" that those who were far off can be brought near, as St. Paul says (Ephesians 2:13). The Saviour of the world does not draw the nations to Himself simply by going to them and teaching them, as the Greeks expected and desired. He draws them to Himself through the "expiation by his blood," through the one atoning act by which men are reconciled to God and thereby to one another.

The Epistle to the Ephesians, to which reference has already been made, shows us the Church as the new household of God, in which those who were formerly strangers have been made children, "reconciled in one body through the cross" (Ephesians 2:16). The same epistle goes on to show the mystery of God's plan, not only to reconcile Jew and Gentile in one body, but also through the same body to manifest to the world "the manifold wisdom of God" (Ephesians 3:7-10).

The Church is thus, according to God's purpose, both the fruit and the sign of God's atoning work. By the deed wrought once for all on Calvary, there is accomplished an atonement so deep and all-embracing, that the deepest divisions between men are transcended, and a body is created in which men of every sort and kind are drawn together. This body is the body of Christ, the new man, the Last Adam. It is not distinguished from the rest of mankind by any peculiarities of race, or tradition, or education, or temperament; it is just mankind re-created in its true image through Him who is the image of God, Jesus Christ. And this body is — in turn — the means through which the many-splendored wisdom of God is mirrored forth in the world, not only to men and nations, but even to the "principalities and powers in the heavenly places."

Such is the picture which St. Paul draws of the Church. It is sometimes argued that this is really a picture of a sort of ideal church and does not apply to the actual human societies which we call churches. This doctrine com-

7

pletely subverts the plain meaning of the text and introduces a wholly false and unbiblical set of ideas in place of the meaning of the apostle. There is no trace in his writings of a distinction between "ideal" and "real." He is talking about the churches that he is writing to in Asia Minor and elsewhere. They are the new household which God has created through Christ in which Jews like Priscilla and Aquila, and Greeks like Luke, and men of mixed origin like Timothy, were actually being knit together in one fellowship. They are the living fruit of the Saviour's promise that He, being lifted up, would draw all men to Himself. They have been drawn together in Him, and now He uses them to draw others. Thus the Good Shepherd gathers His own sheep to Himself, that they may be one flock under one Shepherd.

We are very familiar with the fact that the world has become — in our day — one neighborhood. No part of the world today is as far away from any other as London was from York two hundred years ago. But this propinquity only makes us more acutely aware of the fact that propinquity is not unity. The question "How can men live together in unity?" has become terrible and inescapable. The ideologies by which men try to unify the world become themselves the most fearsome causes of strife. There is no place at which mankind can receive the gift of unity except the mercy-seat which God has provided. We can only be made one at the point where our sins are forgiven and we are therefore enabled to forgive one another. There is no other place where "righteousness and peace have kissed each other." Every other righteousness becomes self-righteousness, and every other peace becomes appeasement. Only He who is lifted up from the earth can fulfill the promise to draw all men to Himself.

Of that promise the Church is the fruit and the instrument. The disunity of the Church is a denial of the promise and a contradiction of the purpose for which the Church is sent into the world. How can the Church give to the world the message that Jesus is able to draw all men to Himself, while it continues to say, "Nevertheless, Jesus is not able to draw us who bear His name together"? How will the world believe a message which we do not appear to believe ourselves? The divisions of the Church are a public denial of the sufficiency of the atonement.

It is of the mercy of God that He has not

allowed our sin wholly to thwart His purpose, and that even in our divided state He permits us to bear some fruit. But what shall we say of those who point to the fruit as a ground for boasting of the divisions? Shall we continue in sin that grace may abound? "Do you not know," says St. Paul, "that God's kindness is meant to lead you to repentance?" When we have understood God's purpose for the Church as it is shown to us in Scripture, there is only one thing to do about our divisions; it is to repent of them, to go — all of us — humbly to the mercy-seat and ask the Lord Himself to show us where we have gone wrong and what we must do to end this scandal. None of us knows exactly what we ought to do, exactly what kind of unity He wants for us. Only He can show us. But we do know — unless we shut our eyes — that these divisions are contrary to His will, and that we ought to repent of them and turn together to Him. When we do that, He will surely use us to fulfill His purpose of drawing all men to Himself.

II.

BY ONE SPIRIT

By one Spirit we were all baptised into one body — Jews or Greeks, slaves or free — and all were made to drink of one Spirit.
                                        —I Corinthians 12:13

HERE you have the dimensions of the Church's being set forth in their barest simplicity. The material — all sorts and conditions of men, Jews or Greeks, slave or free, mankind in all its variety; the form — one body marked off from the world by the act of baptism; the agent — one mighty Spirit, the Spirit of God.

First, then, the Church is a body that contains all sorts and conditions of men. It is not a segregation but a congregation. It is not for men of a particular sort, or race, or temperament, or culture; it is for man as man — or rather for man reborn as child of God. It is simply the home for the whole human race, wherein all men of every kind will be able to say, "This is my Father's house." Nothing human ought to be alien to the Church except sin. It is the one place where every human distinction is transcended and where mankind is restored to its proper character as one family.

As a missionary in India I have often been asked: "Are you really so narrow-minded as to think that you are going to enroll the whole human race in your little group? Are you like the frog that thinks its little pond is the whole ocean?" With all my heart I can answer that I long for every human being to be a Christian. But — in all loyalty to the church of my fathers — I have to confess that I cannot wish for every human being to be a Presbyterian. That is one way of stating the burden which our disunity places on the heart of the evangelist. None of our churches is a big enough fellowship to be a home for the human race. Only a universal fellowship can be the adequate bearer of a universal Gospel. The missionary cannot evade the question: "What is the body which you are asking me to join?" For St. Paul the answer is that it is a body — one body — in which men of every sort and kind are at home. We cannot give that answer, because we represent broken fragments of that body, none of them entitled to make that claim, all of them representing some segment of Christian experience stemming from some limited part of the religious history of the western world. If you stay inside the confines of our western world you can forget that. But if you stand in the streets of a great Asian city to preach the Gospel, you cannot escape facing the question.

But someone may answer: "You are talking about matters of outward organization. These are not the important things. Even though we have these outward divisions, all true believers *are* one body, and share one Spirit. The missionary does not need to be embarrassed by the organizational divisions, which are really unimportant." What would St. Paul have said to this? When he spoke of "one body," was he really just speaking in an ideal or metaphorical sense? Or did he really mean what the words ordinarily mean — one body? Fortunately we do not need to speculate about this, for we have the apostle's own answer. Precisely this problem had arisen in Corinth. The Corinthians seem to have been a very vigorous and enthusiastic body, filled with diverse gifts of the Spirit.

But they had become divided into factions, each taking the name of a leader, Paul, Apollos, or Cephas. There was also (as usually happens in such circumstances) a non-party party, a non-denominational denomination which in effect said, "We disapprove of all your denominations, we are just Christians; we are of Christ."

St. Paul's response to this development must have come as a shock to the Corinthians. He said, "You are yet carnal." The fact that he chose this adjective — the exact opposite of "spiritual" — must have been a shock to them, as it was doubtless intended to be. But it was a carefully chosen adjective. The apostle is telling them that when they begin to develop separate groups based on the name or teaching of particular apostles, they are relying on the flesh instead of the Spirit. He does not mean that they are guilty of lust or other so-called "sins of the flesh." This is not the Biblical understanding of flesh and spirit. He means that they are relying on men rather than on God. To be a Christian means to live the wholly new life which is given when the old life is surrendered at the foot of the Cross. The Christian knows that he is a condemned sinner who has no title to life, much

14

less to glory. His existence is a new gift from God, the life of the Spirit of God given to him through Christ. The only way to describe his life is to say, "Not I, but Christ lives in me." This is the common life in the Spirit, and this is what the Church properly is. But if Christians begin to get together in groups to exalt the name of a particular teacher or leader, to compare themselves with other Christians, and to glory in the things which separate them from other Christians rather than in the Cross which unites all Christians, then — says St. Paul — they are falling back from the life of the Spirit to the life of the flesh. They are falling back into the old world, where men are drawn together into groups and parties by some human teaching or example, instead of living in the new world where men know that they are nothing and Christ is all, where their existence is a daily renewed miracle of grace, and where they dare not glory in anything save in the Cross of Jesus Christ. And St. Paul reminds them that when they were baptized they were not baptized into any part or denomination. They were baptized into Christ — dead and buried with Him and raised with Him — to live henceforth by the power of the one Spirit in one body.

There is, unfortunately, a loose use of the word "spiritual" which enables people in ordinary speech to put asunder the two things which Scripture unites — the one body and the one Spirit. People talk of a "spiritual unity" as something separate from unity in one body. It is often difficult to know what this means. Sometimes it means a feeling of unity which can express itself in occasional courtesies, or in occasional joint demonstrations, but is not strong enough to stand the strain of living together in one body. When people are content with this, feeling degenerates into sentimentality. When Paul speaks about "one Spirit" he is talking about something far removed from this. He is talking of the one Holy Spirit of God given to believers. And he links this indissolubly with "one body," because the proper fruit of the presence of the Spirit of God is a love that is not sentimental but strong and enduring and patient as the love of Christ Himself. Such love expresses itself in more than occasional demonstrations. It expresses itself in a deep and enduring commitment to one another to live as brethren in one family. If we think that a "spiritual unity" which is content with mere feeling and does not seek visible expression in that kind of steady and enduring commitment, is an adequate expression of our unity in Christ, we deceive ourselves.

There is room for much discussion about just what "one body" means for us Christians in the twentieth century. None of us has a clear blue-print for a united Church. We have to ask the Holy Spirit Himself to show us in our own day what visible forms of unity He wills for us. But we have to ask — with penitence and faith. While we continue to boast of our distinctive leaders and doctrines and forms of spiritual life, while we continue to add other names to the One Name, and are not content simply to be called Christians, we come under the Scriptural judgment that we are not spiritual but carnal. Against all our pride in our different traditions there stands the word of the great apostle: "God forbid that I should boast save in the Cross of our Lord Jesus Christ, by which the world has been crucified to me and I to the world."

III.

THAT THE WORLD MAY KNOW

The glory which thou hast given me I have given to them, that they may be one even as we are one, I in them and thou in me that they may become perfectly one, so that the world may know that thou hast sent me and hast loved them even as thou hast loved me.
—John 17:22-23

THIS wonderful prayer of our Lord on the night of His passion is filled with the thought of the glory of God. The words "glory" and "glorify" occur no less than eight times in the chapter. Jesus came into the world to manifest the glory of the Father. And the glory which the Father gave Him is given to those who believe in Him, and through them is to be manifested to the world.

What is the glory which was manifested in Jesus? This same Gospel tells us. "We beheld his glory, glory as of the only Son from

18

the Father" (John 1:14). His glory is the glory of sonship, the glory which is seen in Him who in every circumstance, in the Garden, and on the Cross, could look up to the sovereign Lord of all and say, "Father." In this perfect sonship, the glory of God is manifested. And this is the glory which He gives to those who believe in Him. They receive "power to become children of God" (John 1:12). They too receive this status, this dignity, and this joy, that in every circumstance they can say — as He did — "Father."

The supreme joy of a missionary is to see this glory being given to men, to see those who had been "no-people" receiving the dignity and joy of children of God, and reflecting in new ways and new idioms the manifold richness of God's glory. I have seen this happening among simple village people in South India. I have seen it happening among men serving life-sentences for murder, so that one of them as he went to the gallows was calmly and radiantly bearing witness to his guards and executioners right up to the moment of execution. It is a reflected glory, a glory that shines only because the child of God is always looking into the face of his Father. The sonship is itself the glory.

Our Lord says that He has given this glory to those who believe in Him "that they may be one even as we are one." Being children of God must mean being — in some recognizable sense — members of one family. All our rationalizations of schism and all our evasions of the plain meaning of Scripture will not enable us to side-step the logic of that argument. In some sense those who are children of one Father must be recognizable as members of one family. That is why this wonderful prayer is so filled with longing for the unity of Christ's people — "I in them and thou in me that they may become perfectly one." Those in whom the One Son of God dwells must be one brotherhood, delighting together to honor the one Father.

It has been my privilege during twenty-three years as a missionary in India to serve in two great cities to which hundreds of thousands of pilgrims flock every year to visit the temple. It has been our custom to preach in the streets so that those who come from afar may have the opportunity to hear the Gospel. In the course of such preaching I have often been challenged — perhaps by a well-educated Hindu gentleman who has returned to India after graduating at one of the great British or

American universities. He will put a question something like this: "What right do you think you have to come here with your foreign religion? Do you imagine that you have the whole truth? Do you Europeans suppose that you — with your frightful wars, your hydrogen bombs, and your dirty films and magazines — are in a position to offer spiritual leadership to the world? Can you really think that you, of all people, are entitled to invite the whole world into your fellowship?" The answer to that question must be something like the following: "No, we do not ask you to look at us or to follow us. We ask you to look at Jesus Christ. We are speaking for Him, not for ourselves. We ask you whether there is anyone in all human history to compare with Him, and whether there is any event in all history other than His Cross which can be the place of reconciliation for all mankind. We ask whether there is any other event in all history where the ultimate issues between man and his Maker were exposed and settled. We preach Him as the One Saviour for all mankind." But is it not natural that the questioner should immediately reply: "Yes, that is what you say; but it is not what you believe. For if you believed it, you would yourselves

21

have found it true. You would have found in Jesus a center of unity deep enough and strong enough to overcome your natural divisions and to bring you together as one family. If you really believed that the Name of Jesus is the one name under which all mankind is to be enrolled, you would yourselves have found that Name sufficient. But in fact you add all sorts of other names. Evidently you yourselves do not find in Him the secret that you are offering to us."

That is a challenge which one cannot evade if one is going to go on preaching the Gospel. That is why it is on the mission field that the sense of shame about disunity has been most powerfully at work. It was from the mission fields that the demand for Christian unity came. It was among missionaries that the denominational barriers were first overleaped, and it was the great world missionary conference of 1910 that created the modern movement for Christian unity. The unity of Christ's people, for which He prays, is a unity "that the world may know that thou hast sent me and hast loved them even as thou lovest me." It is a unity for the sake of the world, the world which God made and loves and for which He sent His Son.

These words of our Lord's prayer tell us that there are two things which the world is expected to recognize from the unity of Christians. Firstly, it is to recognize that Jesus has been sent by God. The world is to recognize in the Christian fellowship a supernatural unity, a unity which transcends all the usual human groupings and parties, a unity which is the visible proof of the fact that at the heart of the Christian fellowship there is none other than the Apostle of God Himself; that JESUS is not the name of one of the great human religious leaders, but the name of Him who has been sent by the Creator and Ruler of all as His plenipotentiary for the sake of men. And secondly, the world is to recognize that in the life of the Church the love of almighty God is actually known and experienced. The love of God, the supernatural reality for which the New Testament used the Greek word *agape* instead of any of the ordinary words for human love, is a love which goes beyond any human love and overleaps every human barrier and creates a new kind of fellowship in which men are reborn as members of one family. It is this new reality which the world is to recognize in the Church.

During my visits to the hundreds of small

villages in my old diocese in South India, I was often asked to speak to the non-Christians of the village just before going into the village church to conduct a service with the Christian congregation. I have often stood at the door of a little church, with the Christian congregation seated on the ground in the middle and a great circle of Hindus and Muslims standing around. As I have opened the Scripture and tried to preach the Word of God to them, I have always known that my words would only carry weight, would only be believed, if those standing around could recognize in those sitting in the middle that the promises of God were being fulfilled; if they could see that this new community in the village represented a new kind of body in which the old divisions of caste and education and temperament were being transcended in a new form of brotherhood. If they could not see anything of the kind, they would not be likely to believe.

Today the world has been shrunk to the dimensions of a village. The old separation of cultures has been broken down, and all nations and races are crowded together in closer and closer contact. In the middle of this world God has set His Church as His witness. He expects His Church to be recognizable as

His family. He expects that the glory which He gave to His Son, and which has been given to us, will be visible to the world in the common life of a redeemed brotherhood. He expects that the world will be able to recognize that the Church is the place where His love is actually at work drawing together into one men of every sort and kind.

Because we disappoint that expectation, and flout that loving will, because we present to the world not the one body of Christ, but a terrible series of caricatures, we must repent. The search for Christian unity is thus primarily a matter of repentance. It is not primarily a matter of organization. It is not a matter of the size or number of churches; it is a matter of the meaning of churchmanship. It is a matter of going in penitence and faith to the Lord Himself to ask Him to give us such a common life in His one family that the world may be able to recognize in us the lineaments of the household of God.

IV.

TO ALL NATIONS

Many will come in my name, saying "I am he!" and they will lead many astray. And when you hear of wars and rumors of wars, do not be alarmed; this must take place, but the end is not yet. For nation will rise against nation, and kingdom against kingdom; there will be earthquakes in various places, there will be famines; this is but the beginning of the sufferings. But take heed to yourselves; for they will deliver you up to councils; and you will be beaten in synagogues; and you will stand before governors and kings for my sake, to bear testimony before them. And the gospel must first be preached to all nations.

—Mark 13:6-10

IT HAS become common to say that we live in an age of revolutionary change. It is not as common as it should be for Christians to welcome this fact. Yet surely we should welcome it — not merely because of the challenge which it offers to any man of faith and

26

courage, but because it is precisely what our Lord led us to expect. "I came to cast fire upon the earth and would that it were already kindled!" The events of our time ought not to be strange to us who have the New Testament in our hands. Shall we be surprised or dismayed, as though something unexpected happened? Did anyone really think that so revolutionary an event as the preaching of the Gospel of the crucified Messiah could fail to produce revolutionary effects?

It is a plain fact that much of the ferment of our time can be traced directly to the new contact of the ancient peoples of Asia and Africa with the ideas which have been brought forth into the world from the womb of western Christendom. It is no accident that the newly-liberated people of these continents, having thrown off the colonial tie, do not and cannot go back to the conceptions of human life, of government, of human rights, with which the white man found them. It is no accident that they think now in terms of fundamental human rights, of human dignity, of the welfare state, of freedom from want and fear and the other ills of the world. It is no accident that politics becomes more and more messianic, that leaders and movements arise which promise total welfare for man if he will follow them. These things are what we must expect, for once He who is the Alpha and the Omega, the true origin and the true end of human existence, has appeared, human life can never be the same. It can never return to the static or cyclical patterns of man's pre-Christian history. When Christ has come, men and nations must either give themselves to Him, their true Saviour, or else follow those who offer salvation on other terms. The pressing of this choice to its ultimate issue is precisely the work of Christ — in the days of His flesh, and in the continuing mission of His Church. All history converges upon that choice — the history of every man, and the history of the world. Jesus is the determinative center of all history, as He is its beginning and its end. The ultimate question is, "Faith in Jesus, or unbelief?" And it is the task of the Church, by faithful witness to Him who is the Word of God, sharper than any two-edged sword, to be His instrument in bringing all men and all nations to that choice. Hence, the promise of conflict, of suffering, and of division. "These things must come to pass."

If we understand the dimensions of our task in the terms of the New Testament, we shall be delivered from much of the anxiety which we find around us. We shall not ask, "What is coming to the world?" because we know Who is coming. We shall not think of our task as one of trying to hold back the revolution of our time, but as one of bearing witness within that revolution to its true meaning. We shall not allow ourselves to be so obsessed by the fear of communism that we can see nothing else. Communism is not the author of the revolution of our time; it is one of the movements which exploits it; the revolutionary movement of our time has deeper roots and a wider meaning than communism understands. Our privilege as Christians is to understand its real meaning. The penalty of allowing our judgment to be controlled by the fear of communism is that we may find ourselves defending injustice against the human cry for justice, and tyranny against the cry for freedom. For civilizations as for individuals, the beginning of wisdom is to fear God more than we fear death or disaster or anything else. If God has permitted communism to gain a measure of world power and thereby to threaten our security, that is for His own good reasons. He knows what we need. Our concern is with something far more glorious and far more terrible than anything which any earthly power can either promise or threaten. We have seen the one real crisis of human history, the Cross, the point at which — once and for all — the ultimate issues between man and his Maker were exposed and settled. We know, therefore, the true dimensions of human history. We know that the meaning of all history is the pressing to its final issue of the single question: Christ or anti-Christ? It is the supreme privilege of the Church to be used as God's instrument to press home that issue upon every man and every nation. If in the exercise of that privilege God leads us through suffering, failure, and contempt, that will not surprise us.

Of the many stories I was told in the Congo when I was there in October, 1960, one that remains in my mind is of a young Roman Catholic nun who was left behind in a small town after all other white people had fled. For two days she cried, and finally sent a message to her superior to ask, "What do I do?" The answer came back, "You stay and if necessary you die." She stopped crying and went on with her work. Is that too harsh? It would not be counted so in an earthly warfare.

Our warfare is not less serious, and a servant is not greater than his Lord.

Am I wrong if I say that we have tended to think of missions as one of the good causes which we support, an extra which we attend to after the budget for essentials has been served, something that comes under the head of benevolences, something that you might perhaps pull out of if it isn't going too well? This is false in two ways.

Firstly, it is false because it fails to acknowledge that the Church's mission to the nations is the clue to the real meaning of world history. It is not just a good cause which we have to promote; it is the witness to all mankind of what God is doing and will do, of His kingly power which is hidden now but will in the end be revealed to all in its majesty, glory, and terror. We do not need to waste our time being anxious about whether God's Kingdom will come; what we have to be concerned about is whether or not we are being faithful witnesses to it now, whether when the Lord comes we will be found awake and alert. Secondly, it is false because it means that we have not really faced the question of the truth of the Gospel for ourselves. If the Gospel is just the way of understanding religion which

31

is meaningful for me, which helps me and comforts me, then I have no right to interfere with others who have their own versions of it, their own ways to such peace and security as men can hope for. But the Gospel is the truth, and therefore it is true for all men. It is the unveiling of the face of Him who made all things, from whom every man comes, and to whom every man goes. It is the revealing of the meaning of human history, of the origin and destiny of mankind. Jesus is not only my Saviour; He is the Lord of all things, the cause and cornerstone of the universe. If I believe that, then to bear witness to that is the very stuff of existence. If I think I can keep it to myself, then I do not in any real sense believe it. Foreign missions are not an extra; they are the acid test of whether or not the Church believes the Gospel.

I have used the phrase "foreign missions" — many Christians do not like it. It has overtones of the nineteenth century, of paternalism and colonialism. That is true, and we have to recognize it. There are things in the old missionary pattern which have to be changed and are being changed. It is no longer a matter of the white man going from his advanced civilization to under-devel-

oped areas as the man with the "know how"
going to give it to the rest of the world. It is
a matter of the witness of the whole people
of God in Asia and Africa and the remotest
islands of the sea equally with that of the
peoples of the old Christendom. And we of
the white race will by no means be the domi-
nant partners. We have very much to learn
of Christ from the Christians of Asia and
Africa. I am often shocked by the evidence
that even in well-informed church circles
there is still so little conception of the quality
and quantity of Christian leadership in the
so-called younger churches. The Church of
South India, in which I serve, has nine hundred ordained clergy. Less than 10 per cent
of them are foreign missionaries. By any
standards, there are cities of Europe far more
pagan than some of the cities of Asia and
Africa. The churches of Asia have already
two hundred foreign missionaries sent out
from their own lands to take the Gospel to
others. The home base of foreign missions is
in every place where the Church is, and the
mission field is in every place where Jesus is
not acknowledged as Lord. We need and we
must expect and welcome the witness of Christians from other lands in face of the new

paganism of Europe and America, just as they need and welcome and expect our witness in face of theirs.

Yes, there is much in the old pattern of missions that has to change. But there is much that does not change. What does not change is this: that to be a Christian is to believe that Jesus is the Sovereign Lord and Saviour of all mankind. And to believe that, in any real sense, is to be committed to the Church's mission to all the nations.

The Church's mission to all the nations — that phrase, of course, means more than what we call foreign missions. It means the total corporate witness of the churches and of all who profess and call themselves Christians to the sovereign love of God in Jesus. It includes, for instance, the works of relief in times of emergency, of service to refugees, of aid to stricken and suffering churches, which form such a great chapter in the Christian history of our time. It means also more than this. If we have the New Testament as our guide, we shall understand that the Church's mission concerns nothing less than the fulfillment of God's purpose for the whole life of mankind, for the social structures in which man's life is lived, and even for the cosmos itself. The language of the New Testament is quite clear about this. God's purpose revealed in Christ concerns the whole creation.

I think that means, among other things, that we must make a much bigger effort than we have done, to bring the great issues of international politics, of economic policy, of commercial development, within the range of our thinking about the mission of the Church. It is not enough, for instance, that we should dispense charity on a vast scale to the poor and hungry of the world. It is a great and noble thing, new in its scale and its vision, but it is not enough. Charity is greater than justice, but it is never a substitute for justice. We have, I believe, reached a stage in human history where we must bend our minds to the task of devising those economic and fiscal policies which will enable something like economic justice to be established among the peoples; to the creation of a situation in which the Indian or African peasant who labors all day in the sweat of his brow will not be rewarded by a mere pittance, while the same day's labor of a man in Western Europe, or Australia, or America produces the equivalent of a month's earnings in Asia. This task calls for the kind of dedicated and adventurous thinking which has, inside many of the western nations, abolished in our time the same kind of injustice between rich and poor. It calls also for costly ~~and unpopu~~lar decisions in the realm of public policy. In both of these, Christians should surely be in the lead.

I have mentioned this as one aspect — I believe a very important one — of the Church's mission to the world in its broadest sense, but I choose now to speak of the missionary task in its more restricted sense, in the sense of those operations which are designed to take the Gospel to those who do not know Christ or do not acknowledge Him. I have recently returned from spending two months in Africa, visiting in fifteen different territories, and consulting with groups of African and missionary churchmen about the task of the Church in the light of the Word of God and of the needs of Africa today. I want to share with you three deep impressions which that experience has left with me.

(1) In the first place, I have been told by African churchmen what they expect from us in the way of missionary help. They want men and women who will come to Africa ready to be completely part of the Church there, ready to sink their lives in its life. "Send us

missionaries," they said, "who will live with us, work with us, die with us, and lay their bones here in Africa." Over and over again they said they did not want missionaries who thought of themselves as scaffolding for the African Church. Indeed, they said, "We do not want an African Church, we want a Christian Church in Africa, a Church which is truly missionary, and in which there is neither black nor white." A distinguished pastor in the Republic of Cameroun said, "The missionary in the Church should be like salt in the meat. He should lose himself in the Church." A few days later, a Congolese pastor put it that the missionary should be the sugar in the coffee. I leave it to you to decide which you prefer; the point is the same. Africa and the world need men and women who will be ready to commit their lives without reserve to partnership in the Gospel with Christian people in every part of the world.

(2) A second impression was made in my mind more slowly, but not less deeply, as the African journey went on. It was this. We have been concerned, and rightly concerned, with the needs of the so-called under-developed areas for education, health, and aids of all kinds. We have been concerned that mis-

sionaries should be equipped to play their part in giving them this aid, and this too is right. But I found myself increasingly aware, and candid African churchmen confirmed the impression, that there is also a danger here, a danger of losing the one essential thing for which the missionary movement exists. That one essential is the Gospel of the saving power of God in Jesus Christ. That Gospel we share with our African Christian brethren. In respect to the Gospel, we are co-partners. When we speak of under-developed areas, we are using a criterion which *we* have devised. If we take our measuring rod from the New Testament, who shall say which are the under-developed areas? Some of the brethren of the revival movement whom I met in East Africa, the people who had faced horrible death rather than give way to racial hatred, had so little education that we could not converse in any European language. But in their company, I knew that if there was anybody under-developed, it was myself. And one of them, a man of the highest education in the culture of the western world, gently reminded us that if missionaries speak too much about technical gifts and skills, the wealth and the resources which they can bring, a new kind of paternalism can easily be created and the real gift of the missionary to the Church be lost. There are many kinds of inter-church aid, and we must be thankful for them all. But we must beware of thinking of inter-church aid only in terms of the things in which we are strong — wealth, education, technical skill. If we do that, we shall lose the real mutuality, the real equality, which St. Paul says should belong to all the members in the body of Christ. There is a sense in which a missionary who goes out from the Church in America to the Church in Africa is an inter-church aid worker, but the essential gift which he brings is his missionary faith and his missionary calling, his experience of the saving power of Christ and his longing to help the Church in Africa and to share that experience more widely. And *that* kind of inter-church aid is one in which there can be real mutuality, in which all can be both givers and receivers, in respect of which it might even happen that some of the under-developed areas were found here among us in the Christian West.

(3) And that brings us to my third impression. The world missionary task of the Church demands all that we have and are —

our wealth, our skill, our strength. And yet, my strongest impression at the end of this journey in Africa is that the things most needed are the things no money can buy. Here one has to say things that may sound impractical but are yet the real truth. Karl Barth once wrote that when God speaks to us we don't want to wait to hear Him to the end, but jump up to drown His voice with our good works. It would be easy to end with a great call for missionary advance, and yet that might just be the way of shutting our ears to God's Word. There are times when God speaks hard words to His Church. To one which was apparently prosperous, He sent this message:

> You say I am rich, I have prospered, and I need nothing; not knowing that you are wretched, pitiable, poor, blind, and naked. Therefore, I counsel you to buy from me gold refined by fire, that you may be rich . . . (Revelation 3:17-19).

Could it be that this is His word to our strong and prosperous churches in Europe and America today? There is gold to be had — refined by fire — if we want it. We have to ask it from Him, and He chastens those whom He loves.

We do not need to be anxious about His cause. Nations and empires are but the small dust of the balance before Him. He is the First and the Last, the Living One, in whose hand are the keys of death and hell. His cause is not in doubt. What matters is that we would know Him, know that there is none to be feared beside Him, none to be loved except Him, nothing to be desired beside Him; know both the fellowship of His suffering and the power of His resurrection, both His power and His peace, so that we may be the bearers of His peace to all the nations. We have nothing to fear except God. Jesus knows the weakness of His Church. It was in the moment when He knew it most poignantly that He said:

> The hour is coming, indeed it has come, when you will be scattered, every man to his home, and will leave me alone; yet I am not alone, for the Father is with me. I have said this to you, that in me you may have peace. In the world you have tribulation; but be of good cheer, I have overcome the world (John 16:32-33).

Library of Congress catalog card number, 61-10855

Is Christ Divided?

*A Plea for Christian Unity
in a Revolutionary Age*

by

LESSLIE NEWBIGIN

*General Secretary
International Missionary Council*

*Wm. B. Eerdmans Publishing Co.
Grand Rapids, Michigan*

261.9

David Groh

Baden

Feb, 1964